ALWIN SCHROEDER

170 FOUNDATION STUDIES

for

VIOLONCELLO

Selected and progressively arranged from the foremost instructive works of Buchler, Cossmann, Dotzauer, Duport, Franchomme, Grützmacher, Kummer, Lee, Merk, Piatti, Schroeder, and Servais.

Published in Three Volumes

Volume 1   (O2469)
Volume 11   (O2470)
Volume 111 (O2471)

CARL FISCHER, Inc.

62 COOPER SQUARE, NEW YORK 10003
BOSTON · CHICAGO · LOS ANGELES

0 8258 0177 X

Preface

In view of the huge amount of study-material available for the Cello, a careful selection of exercises such as the present, supplied with modern fingering, revised bowing and careful adjustment of dynamics, should prove of utmost serviceability and benefit. Various reasons make it desirable during a course of study to possess a handy volume of reference, in which exercises for specialized technical difficulties or intricate bowings may be found and my object in compiling this volume has been to supply such a collection for the express use of teachers and students in search of carefully selected and graded studies chosen from the very best works in existence.

Many years ago, in fact when I was still a teacher at the Royal Conservatory of Music in Leipzic, Germany, I considered the practical advantages of such a collection and seriously determined to prepare one at first opportunity But then I was called to America as first cellist of the Boston Symphony Orchestra, and the manifold duties of this position together with those of my String Quartet and solo engagements, took up my time to such an extent, that all plans for work along instructive lines had to be postponed indefinitely.

However, since my retirement from the orchestra and with more time to dispose of for teaching, interest in many of my former plans was revived and the long-cherished idea of a volume of selected studies was taken up without delay and carried to a practical conclusion in the present publication.

In deciding upon the contents of this volume, my own teaching experience prompted me to include only such studies as would be of utmost benefit and importance in a general course, and while it was impossible to include many others which should have been added, owing to lack of space, I feel confident that the selection as a whole covers a very wide field and will offer no end of possibilities for advancement and musicianly culture to everyone who studies them.

Alwin Schroeder

Contents

VOLUME I.
(Studies 1 to 80)

VOLUME II.
(Studies 81 to 137)

VOLUME III.
(Studies 138a to 170)

19138-I

170 Foundation Studies

for

Violoncello

Progressively Arranged by
ALWIN SCHROEDER

Volume III

(Studies 138ª-170)

———◇○◇———

	ABBREVIATIONS		ABKÜRZUNGEN
⊓	Down-bow	⊓	*Herunterstrich*
V	Up-bow	V	*Hinaufstrich*
Fr.	At the frog of the bow	Fr.	*Am Frosch des Bogens*
M	In the middle of the bow	M	*In der Mitte des Bogens*
Pt	At the point of the bow	Pt	*An der Spitze des Bogens*
W. B.	Whole bow	W. B.	*Ganzer Bogen*
L. H.	Lower half of the bow	L. H.	*Untere Hälfte des Bogens*
U. H.	Upper half of the bow	U. H.	*Obere Hülfte des Bogens*
I	A String	I	*A Saite*
II.	D String	II	*D Saite*
III	G String	III	*G Saite*
IV	C String	IV	*C Saite*

19138

2

138ª

Andante tranquillo

Büchler, Op. 18, Nº 10

19138ᵇ 310

138b

Merk, Op. 11, No 4

4

Vivace

p staccato

cresc.

cresc.

p

cresc.

p

cresc.

19138^b 310

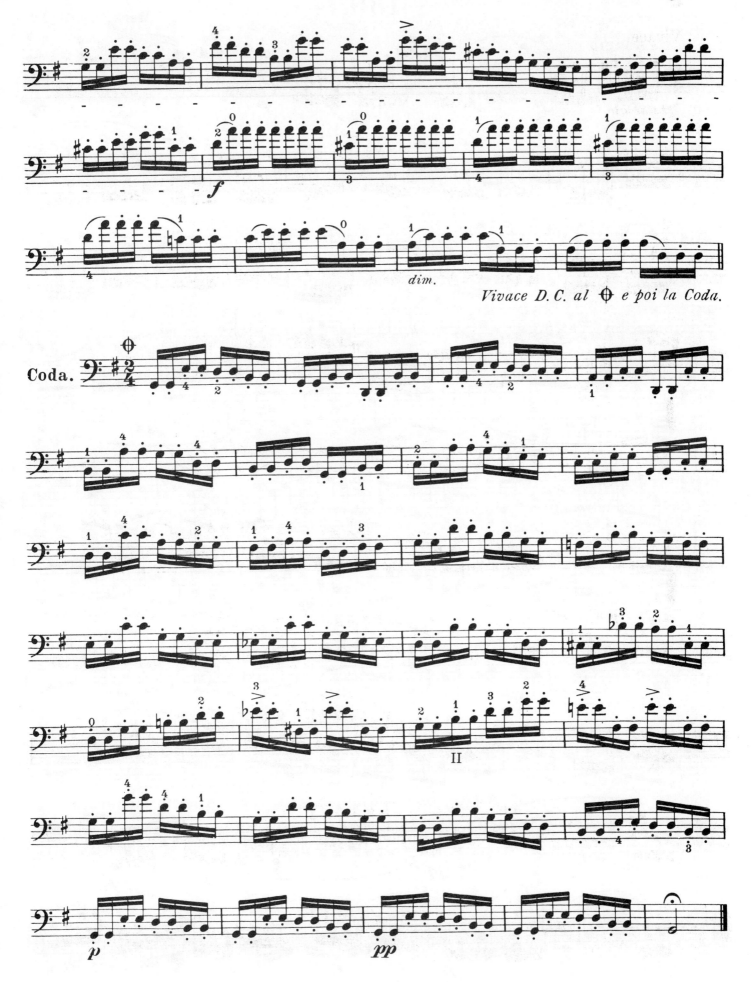

139.

Merk, Op. 11, № 5

140.

Merk, Op. 11, № 6

Adagio

Allegro moderato

141.

Merk, Op. 11, N.º 7

Moderato

U.H.

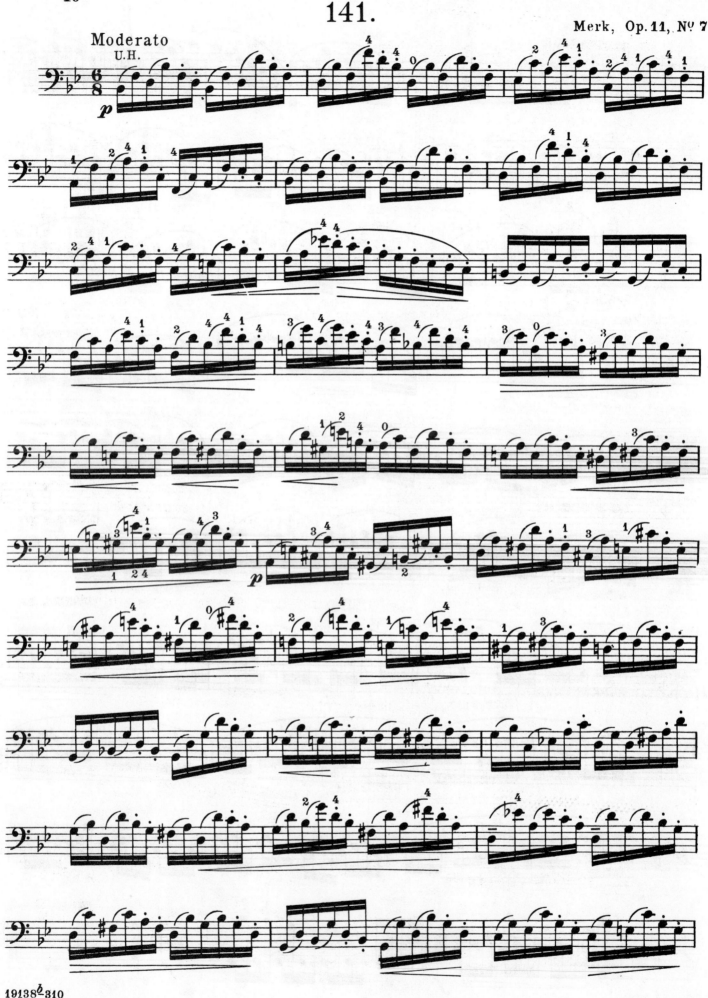

142.

Merk, Op. 11, No 8

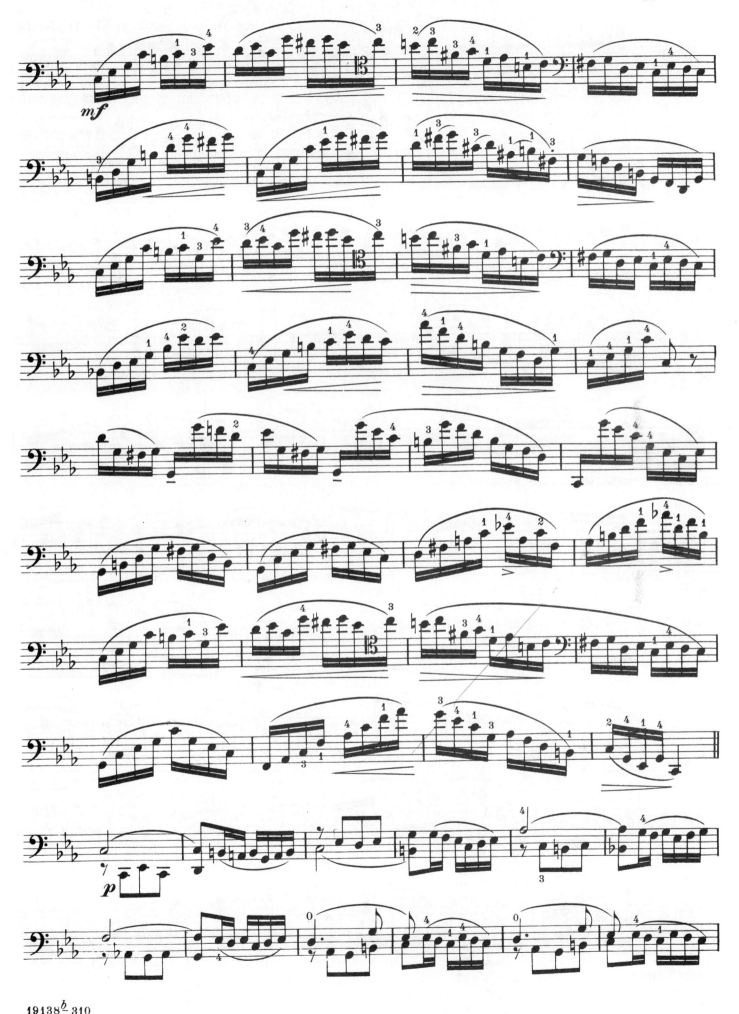

143.

Merk, Op. 11, № 13

16

piùmosso ma non troppo

18

144.

Merk, Op. 11, № 14

Adagio

Allegro ma non troppo

20

Animato più presto

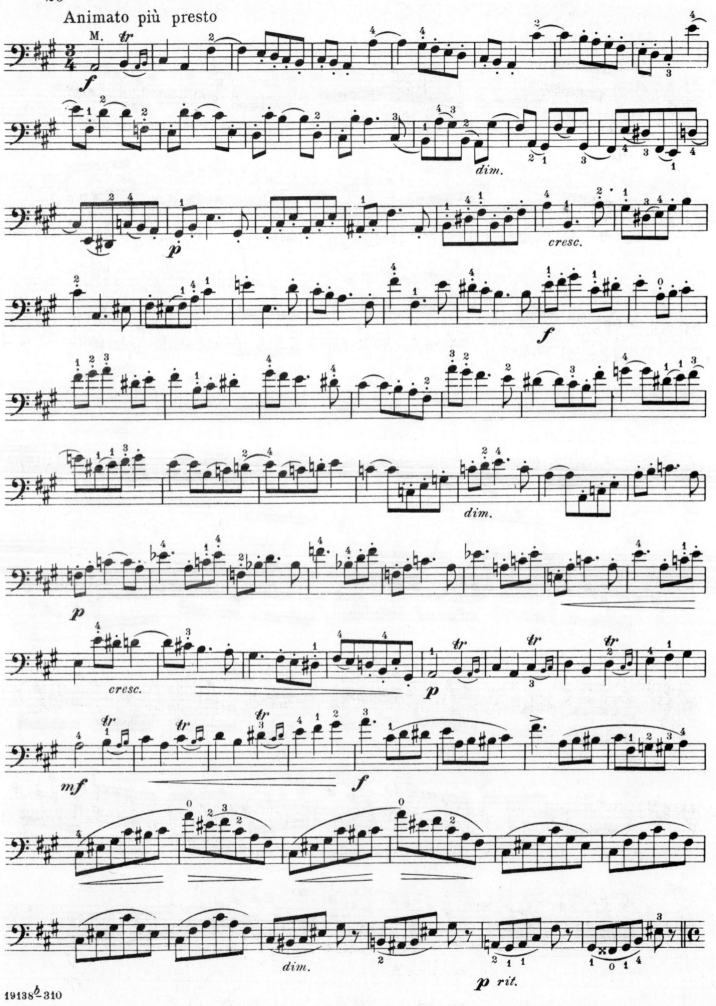

19138b-310

Allegro ma non troppo

145.

Merk, Op. 11, № 15

Allegro con moto

Allegro quasi presto

146.

Alfredo Piatti, Op. 25, Nº 1

19138b 310

147.

Piatti, Op. 25, № 4

148.

Allegro comodo

Piatti, Op. 25, Nº 5

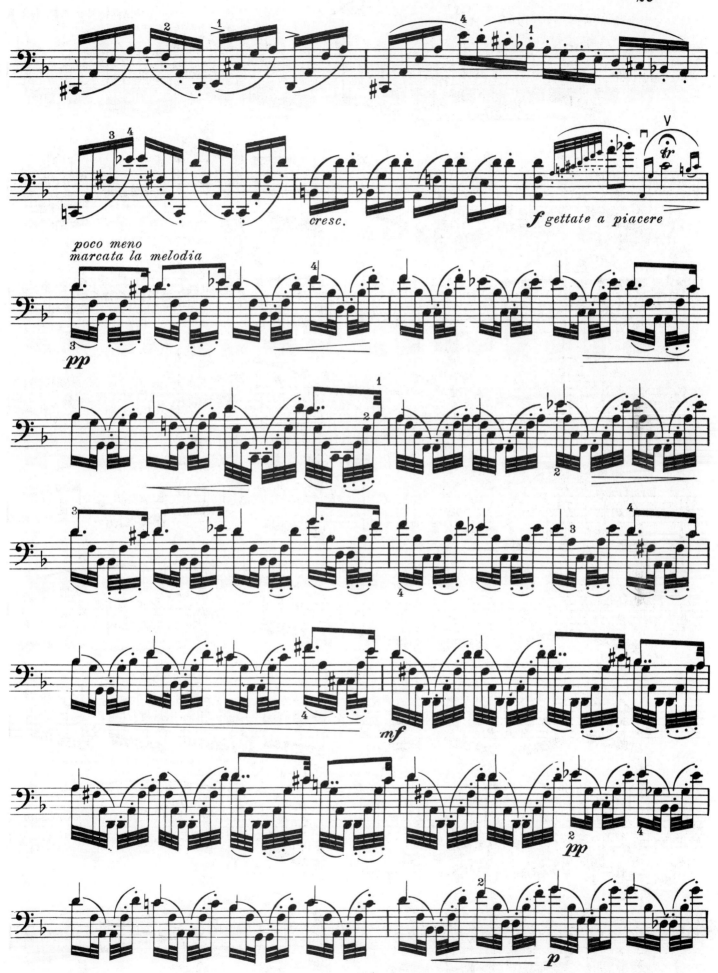

poco meno
marcata la melodia

cresc.

f gettate a piacere

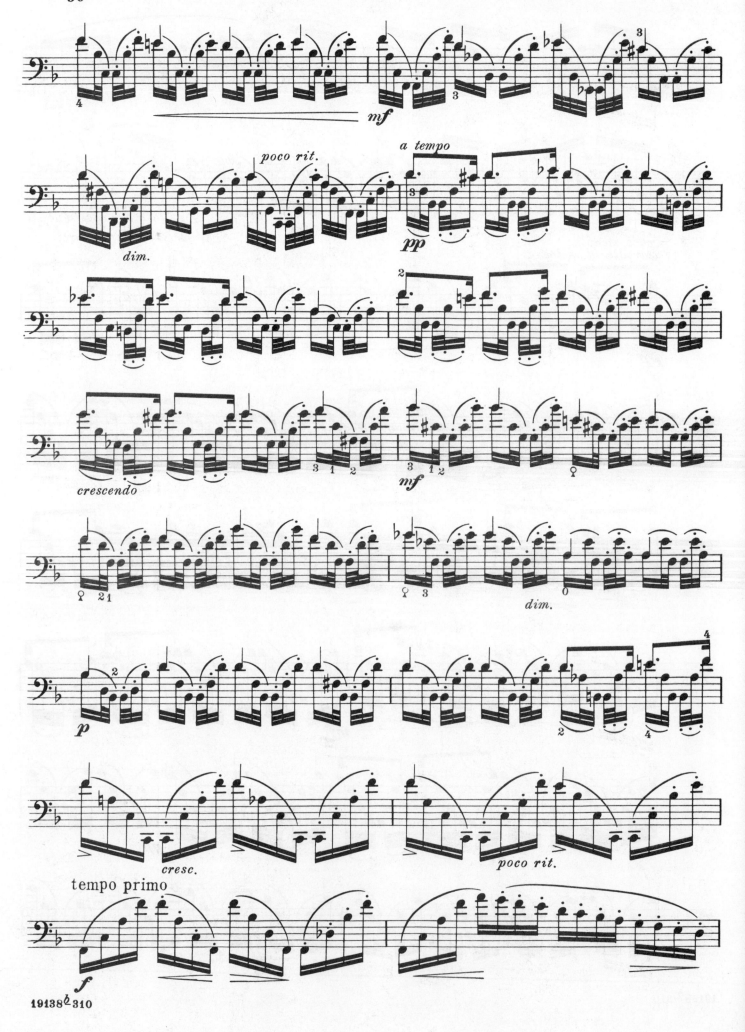

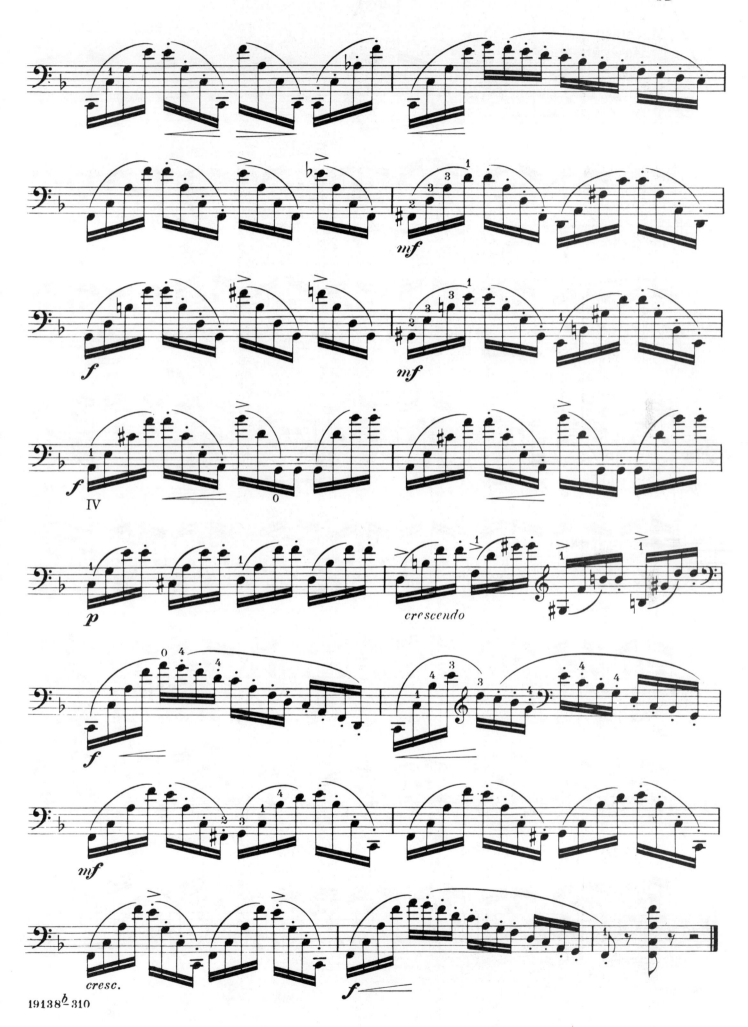

149.

Piatti, Op. 25, No 7

Maestoso

Ben marcato il basso

34

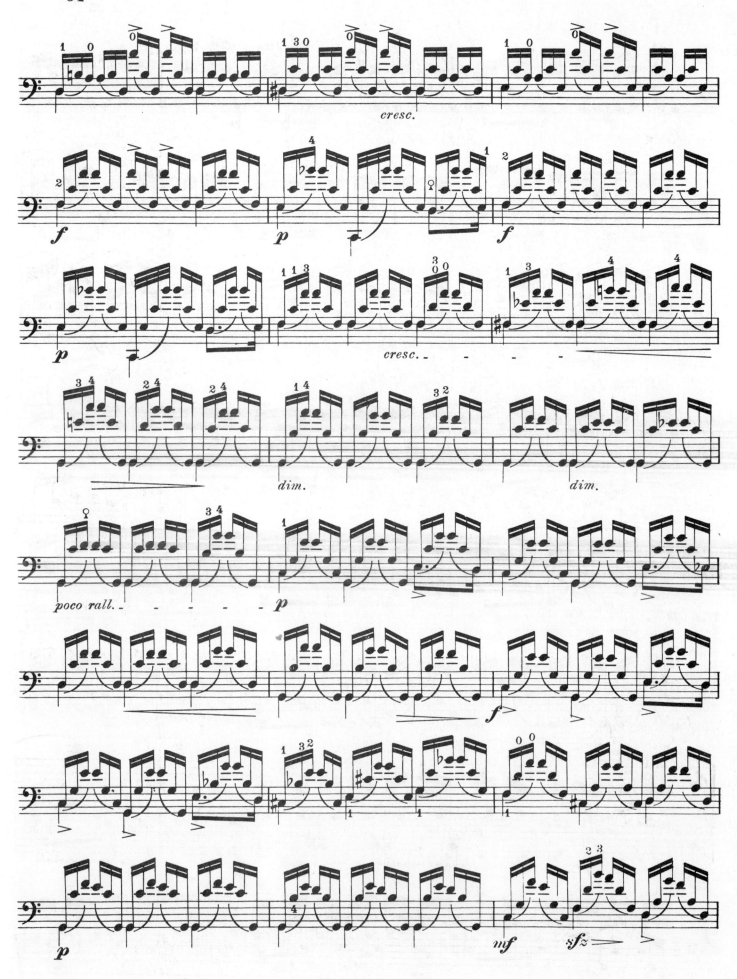

150.

Piatti, Op. 25, Nº 9.

Allegro. *bene spiccato*

151.

Merk, Op. 11, Nº 17

Con allegrezza

40

19138b 310

152.

Merk, Op. 11, N⁰ 18

153.

Allegro ma non troppo
W.B.

Merk, Op. 11, № 19

154.

Merk, Op. 11, N⁰ 20

Maestoso con espressione

Variation 1.

Un poco più lento

Dal 𝄋 al Fine

48

Variation 2.

Variation 3.

155.

Merk, Op. 11, № 16

156.

Allegro moderato

C. Schröder, Op. 57, № 10

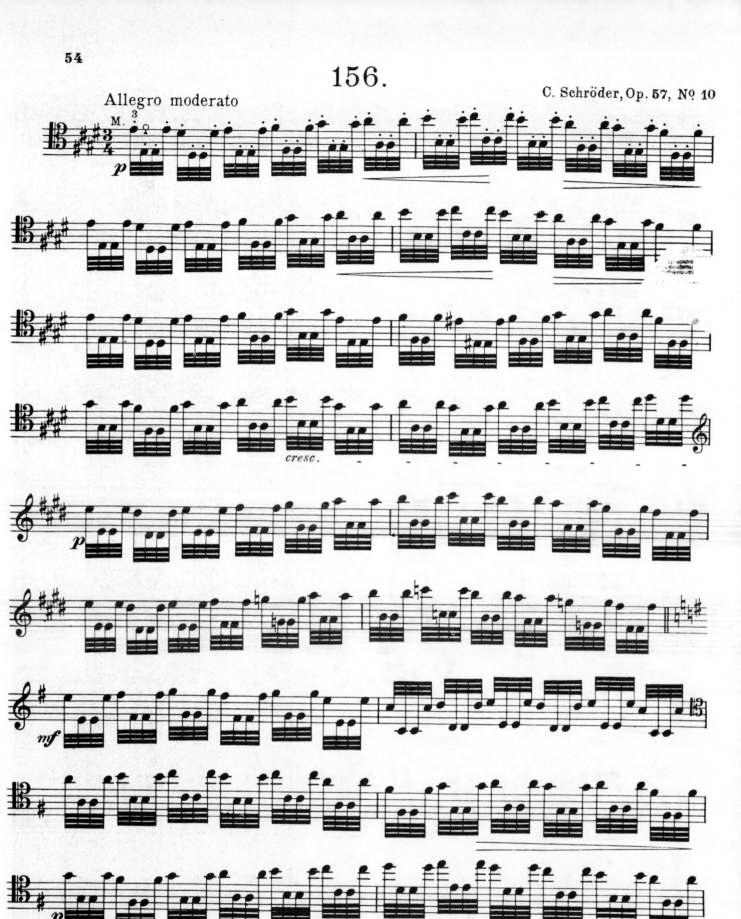

55

pizz.

dim.

diminuendo

19138b-310

157.

Duport

59

19138ᵇ 310

60

158.

Berteau

Allegro

19138 310

159.

Allegro moderato

Duport

Varieties of Bowing

160.

Duport

crescendo

f

dim. è calando   a tempo   f

p

mf

mf

tr   tr

tr   tr   tr

mème Pos.   mème Pos.

f

161.

Cossmann, Op. 10, № 1

Con brio (M. M. ♩ = 126)

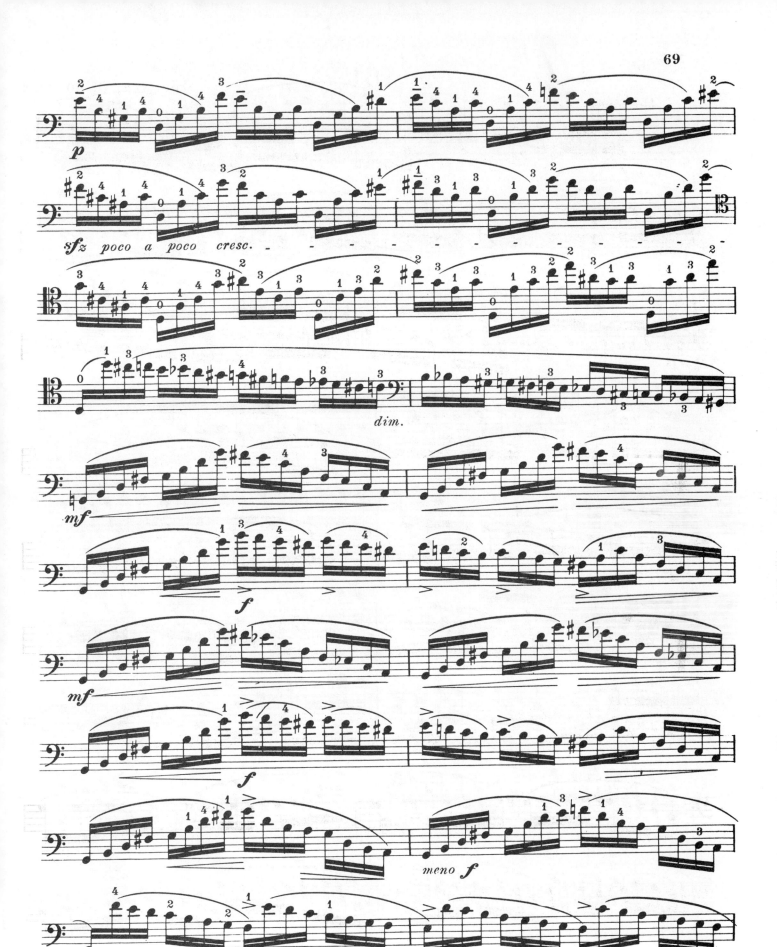

70

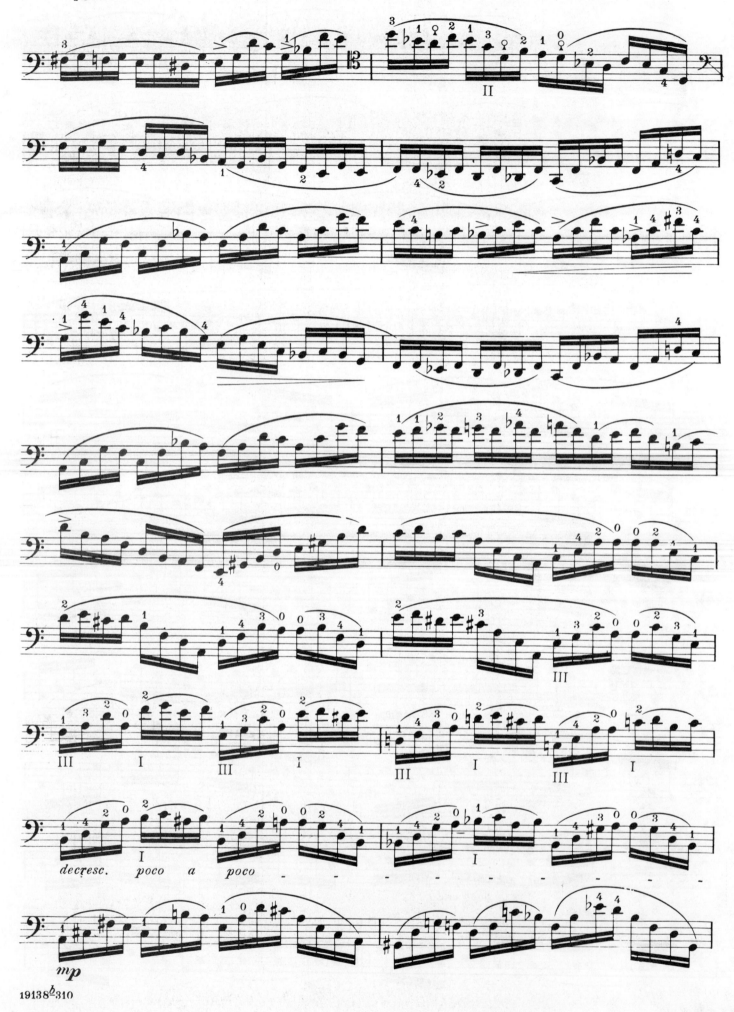

decresc.   poco   a   poco

mp

19138b310

72

19138ᵇ_ 310

II

cresc. poco a poco

f

162.

Tempo moderato (M.M. ♩ = 92)

Cossmann. Op. 10, № 2

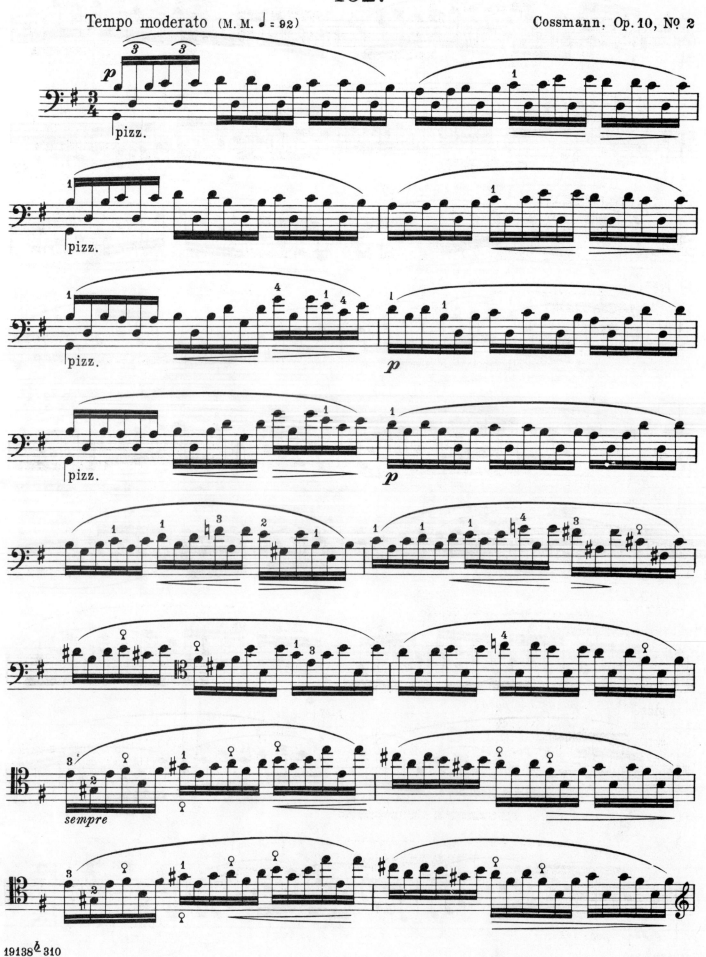

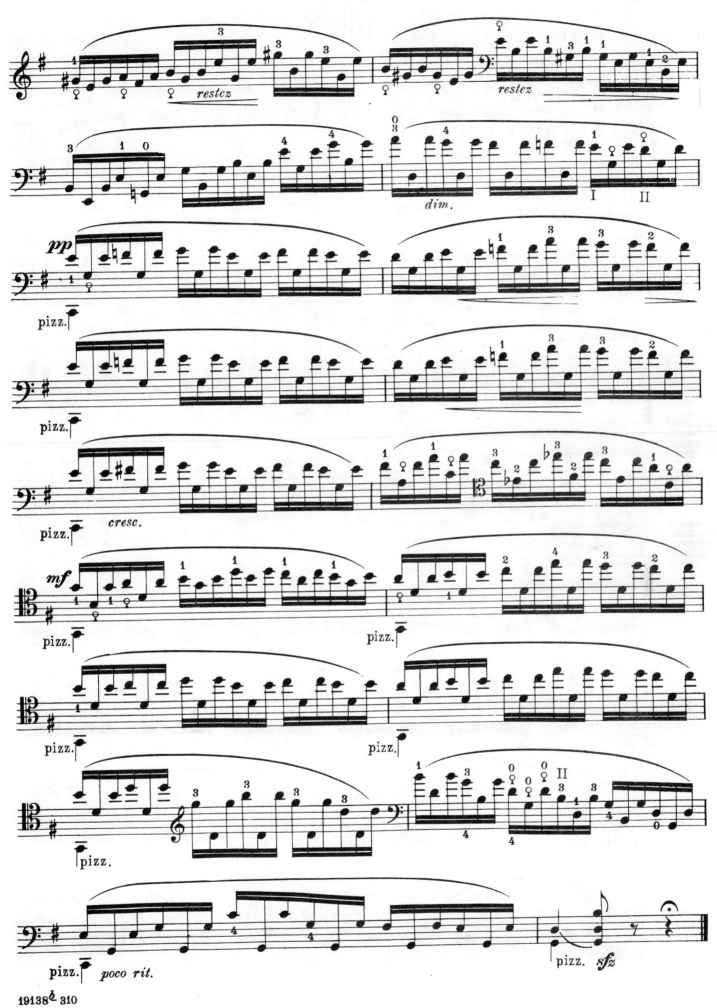

163.

Allegro non troppo (M.M. ♩ = 112)

Cossmann, Op. 10, No 4

78

80

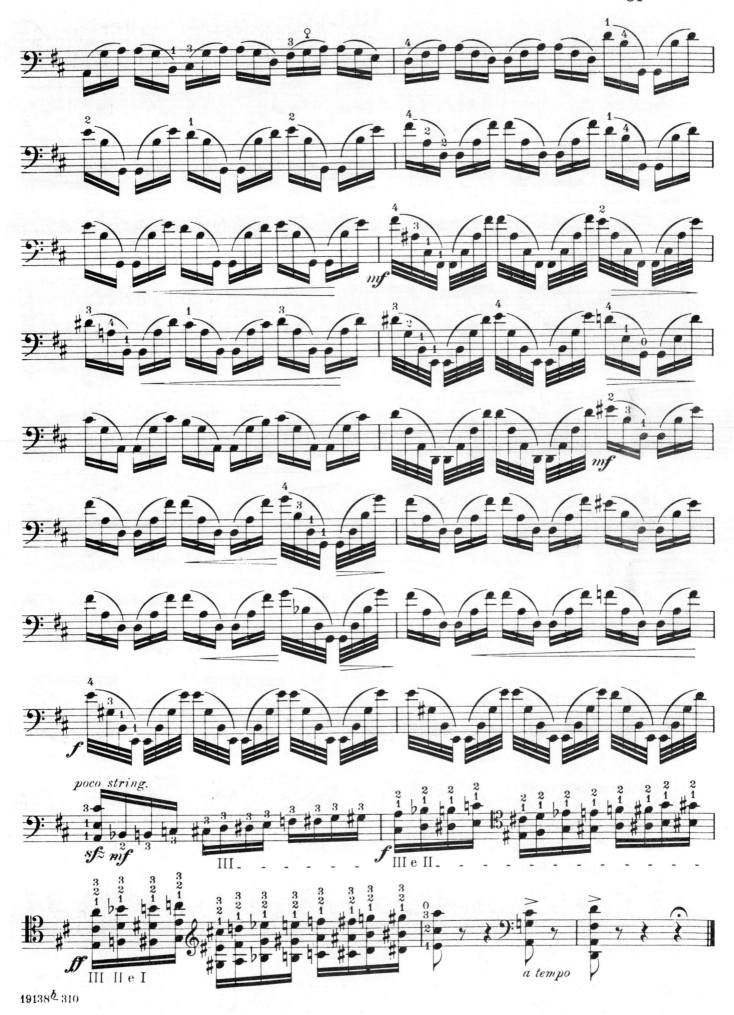

164.

Allegretto ma non troppo

Servais, Op. 11, № 1

Chansonnette Flamande
Tempo Iº

84

19138ᵇ 310

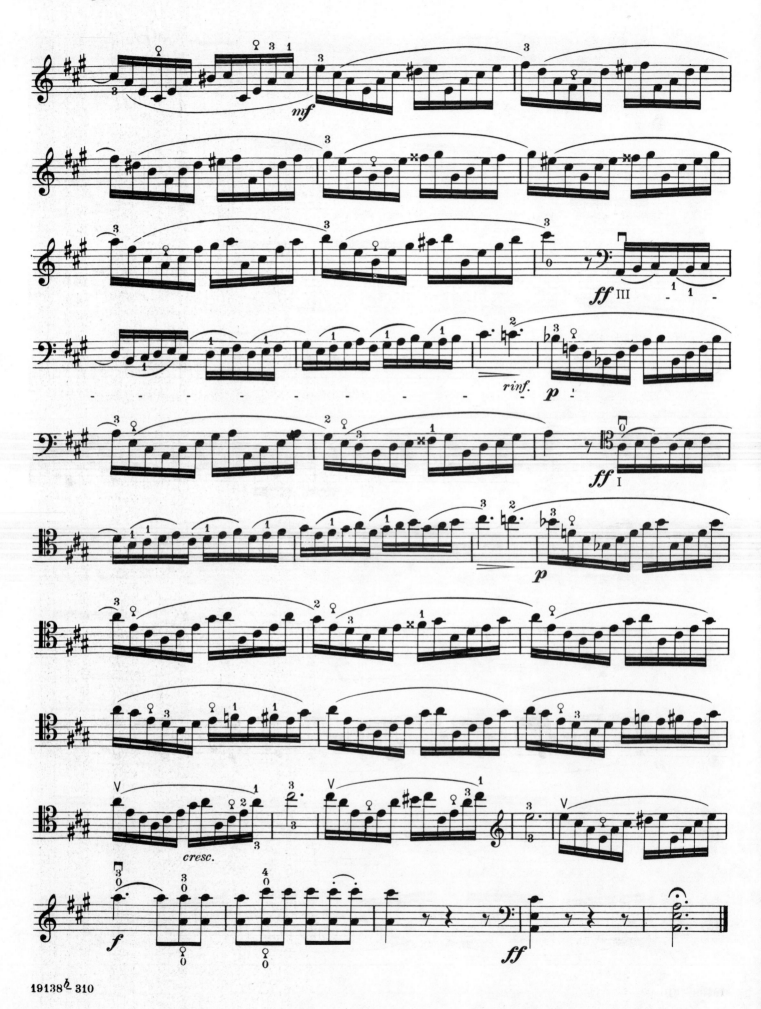

165.

Allegro con moto

Servais, Op. 11 № 2

88

166.

Andante religioso

Piatti, Op. 25, № 2

92

19138ᵇ310

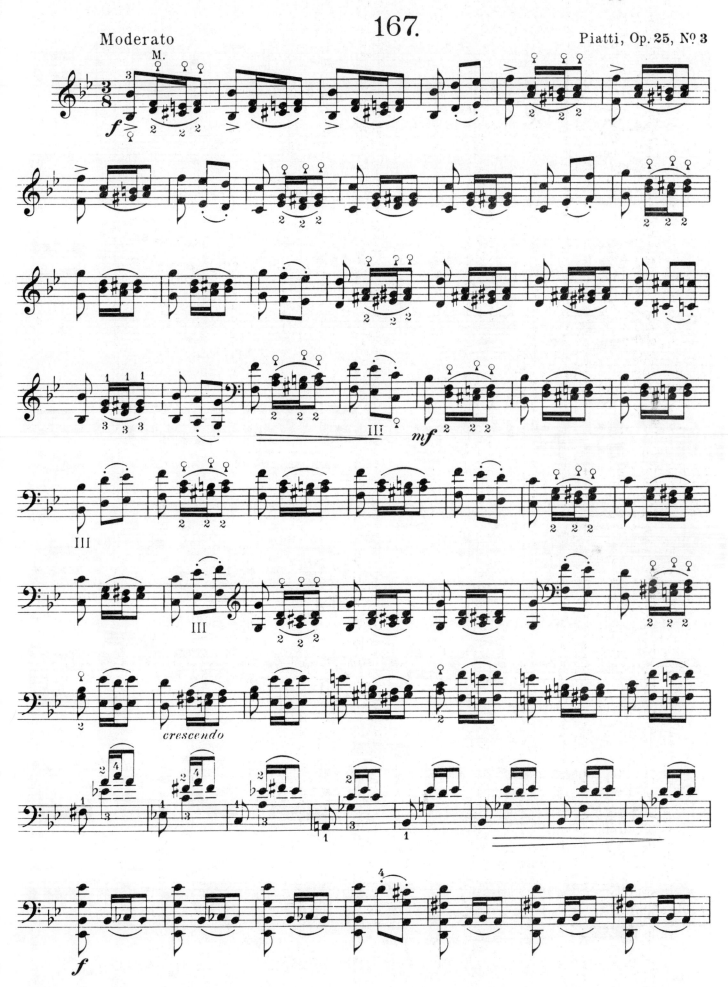

167.

Moderato

Piatti, Op. 25, No 3

94

168.

Piatti, Op. 25, N? 8

Moderato ma energico

169.

Piatti, Op. 25, Nº 10

Allegro deciso

170.

Piatti, Op. 25, Nº 12

Allegretto capriccioso

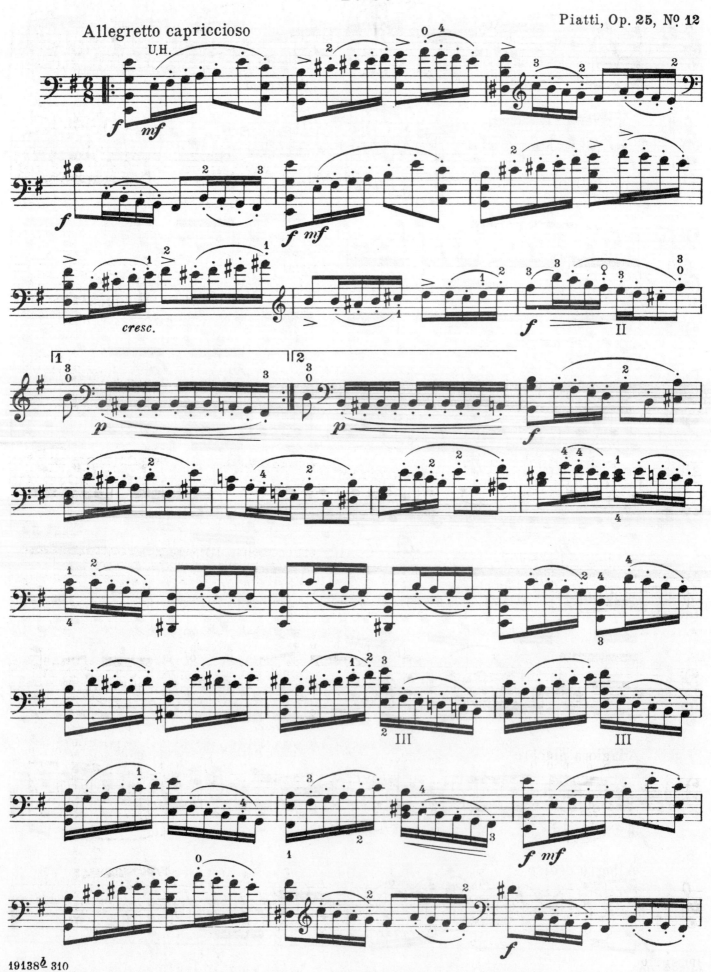

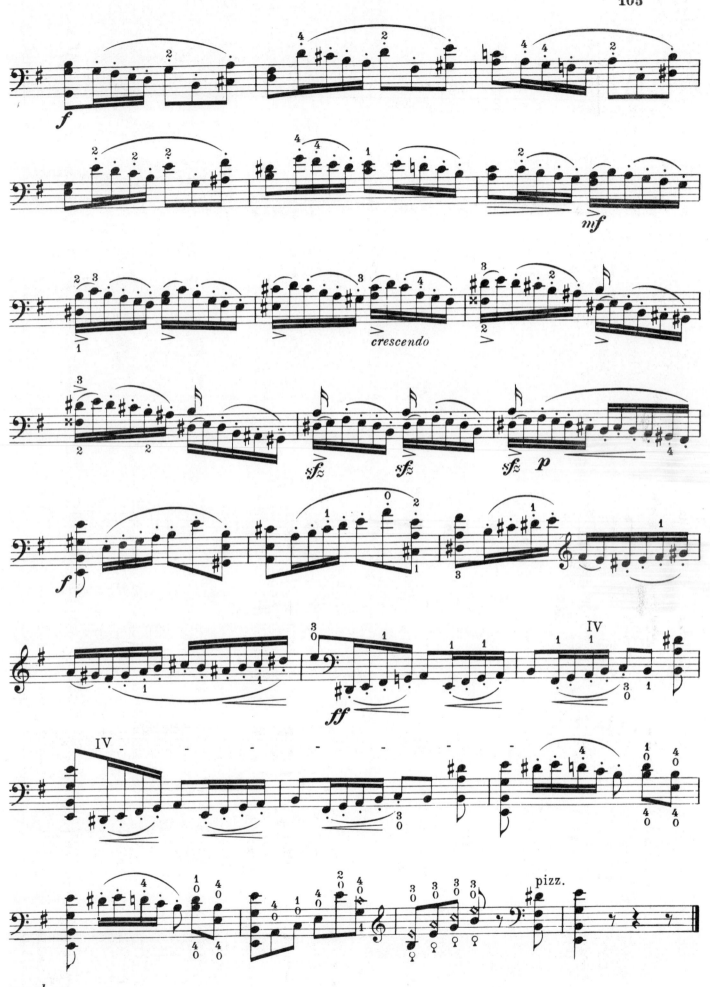